ANGELS

GOD'S HEAVENLY HOST

CHELSEA KONG

Angels

Published in the United States of America

Copyright 2024

Chelsea Kong

ISBN:9781998335664

All rights reserved. No part of this work is transferable, either in whole or in part. It may not be reproduced, stored in a retrieval system, or transmitted in any form or by any means, electronic, mechanical photocopying, recording, or otherwise, without the express prior written permission of both the copyright owner and this publisher. Scanning, uploading, and distribution of this book via any means whatsoever is illegal and punishable by law.

This book is created using stock images from Canva, Adobe, Pixels, and Deposit Photos, and layered in Photoshop.

Everyone has heard about angels. But what are they? Where did they come from? And why are they here?

Angels live forever but some look very young and others may look much older. They are blessed with wisdom and intelligence to help people.

Not all angels look like us. While in the bible there is no specific mention of wings, many other records they do describe them. Some look like light. All were created to glorify and worship God and His son Jesus.

In Revelation 14:6 John says he saw an angel flying in the heavens preaching the everlasting gospel to all that dwell on earth, that God loves the world, has redeemed mankind, and all belong to Him.

While there are many angels in heaven only certain angels are named in the bible. Many are only mentioned by their rank. This is called the Angelic Hierarchy. The Highest Ranks of Angels are the oldest, & most advanced.

Seraphim

The Seraphin are the highest order of angels. They are the closest to the Godhead. They are often called the "Fiery Ones" as they shine or burn with the spiritual fire of God's divinity.

Cherubim

These angels stand second to the throne. They work to make the whole of creation into one harmonized system through wisdom, divine knowledge and the freedom of choice in all matters relating to life.

Thrones

The third rank of angels are described as a wheel within a wheel covered with eyes. Known for their great intelligence, the Ophanim speak directly with God and interpreted his will so it can be used in a practical way.

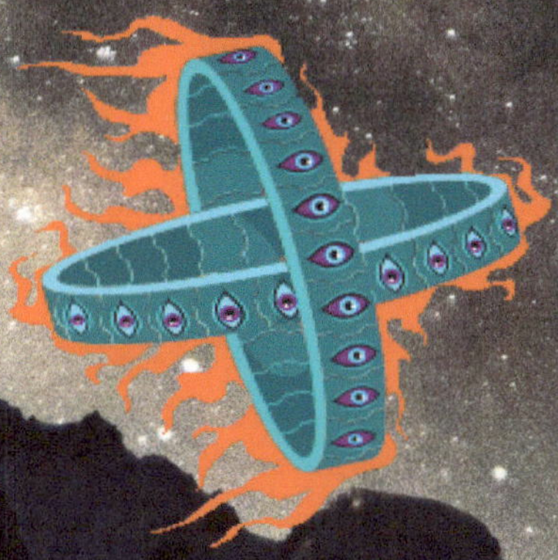

Ophanim

Dominions

The Dominions are also known as the Kyriotetes. These angels oversee the duties of lower angels. Though God's Divine Grace they are blessed with the infinite possibility of creation, and rarely get a chance to meet and talk with humanity.

The Virtues

The Virtues are also known as the Dynamis. These angels of organization are often connected with miracles, and keeping the planets and stars in order. Their level of consciousness is also associated with the willpower to achieve a goal and the courage to take action.

The Powers

Not a lot is known about the angelic beings known as the Elohim or the Powers. As the enforcers and guardians of the Divine Will, they directly monitor and regulate the symmetric order of patterns within time and space. They are believed to act as Gods' magistrates and judges and oversee physical incarnation.

Principalities

As the angelic Principalities, the Archai work within the cycles of time. They are the commanders of the angels and archangels, who fulfill God's orders. They often communicate directly with humanity in order to govern and guide the activities, evolution, and spiritual advancement of nations, churches, and humanity.

Archangels

These great beings of unconditional love act as heralds to bring news, guidance, and an alternative perspective to humanity regardless of religion or culture. They exist outside of time and space and can appear to many people in different locations at the same time. They are able to view all points of reality, including our past, present and future. This enables them to offer powerful guidance and new perspectives. They also oversee the angels who provide help to us on Earth.

Angels

Mankind is most familiar with the angels who work tirelessly to strengthen our connection with God. Throughout time, angels have always been with us. They carry our prayers to heaven and deliver messages of hope. They comfort us when we are sad and help those who ask, even though we may not see them.

Named Angels

While Gabriel, Michael, Lucifer, and Abaddon are the only angels named in the Bible, many more are named in Judiasim in the New Testament (1st century CE) and in rabbinic literature. Gabriel and Michael are the first angels to be named in the Book of Daniel.

Angels often manifest in human form, yet they are described as supernatural beings of emotional and intellectual energy formed through God's will. These malach, or messengers are created to perform a specific task.

Ariel

While only mentioned once in the Bible, (Isaiah 29) Ariel is mentioned several times in Hebrew literature. Known as the lion of God, Ariel serves to heal, guard, guide and helps man learn God's plan.

The angel Ariel guards and brings healing to the plants and animals of the earth. Ariel is also associated with the health and wellbeing of the natural elements : air, fire, water and soil.

Azrael

Know as the one through which God helps, Azreal or Azriel is said to seek justice for the dead who were wronged during life. He is said to guide the souls of the dead to their afterlife.

As the Angel of Death, Azreal is said to have appeared to Peter before his death. Other stories say he appears to all saints to allow them time to prepare for their death. Genesis 32:24 and Exodus 12:23 & 24

Chamuel

One of seven archangels that stand in Gods presence, he is often called the angel of strength and love. He brings the message of God's love for all and is said to heal broken hearts.

He is said to be the angel who comforted Adam and Eve after they were driven from Eden, and was the angel with Jesus in the Garden of Gethsemane, before he was crucified. Daniel saw him before writing his prayer for Israel.

Daniel 10: 13-21

Gabriel

His name means Man of God and God is my strength. He is the herald of the Almighty and brings news and revelation of his word. He appeared to Daniel to help him understand his visions.

Gabriel was the first named angel in the Bible. He appeared to Mary to bring the news that through the power of the Holy Spirit, she would bear Jesus Christ, the long awaited Savior.

Haniel is often listed as one of the seven angels that stand near God. The angel of creativity, inspiration, wisdom, and new ideas, Haniel represents the nurturing, artistic, and loving aspects of life.

Jeremiel

The arch angel Jeremiel, also known as Eremiel is often called the Gatekeeper, as he watches over and guides the holy deceased to Heaven. In Hebrew his name is "God shall have mercy."

As the angel of emotions he helps us open up about things we seek to hide, and take an inventory of our thoughts and emotions to bring about a positive change. He also carries messages of frustration or troubles to God.

Jopiel

The archangel of Joy, Learning and Creativity is also known as Yopiel. The name means Beauty of God and she is said to be the companion of Metatron. She is often depicted with a scroll in hand.

Jopiel teaches beauty through art and music. At the dawn of creation she was the teacher who taught 70 languages to the new souls. Jopiel imparts divine wisdom to provide guidance and allows you to see all options clearly in life .

Metatron

No one is certain how the angel got his name. One story is he is Enoch after God took him. Genesis 5:24 His name means one who stands behind the throne. This fits as he is described as the Scribe and record keeper of Heaven who records the good deeds people do and guards the Tree of Life.

Metatron listens to prayers and records our spiritual choices in the Book of Life. Many call him the voice of God and see a flash of light or the scent of strong herbs and spices in his presence. In the book of Jude he is cited as a prophet. 1:14-15

His first role is the leader of the Army of God, and is known for his fight with Satan, Israel's accuser, who was cast from Heaven. He is known as the Champion of Israel, and destroyed Sennacherib's army during the Exodus from Egypt.

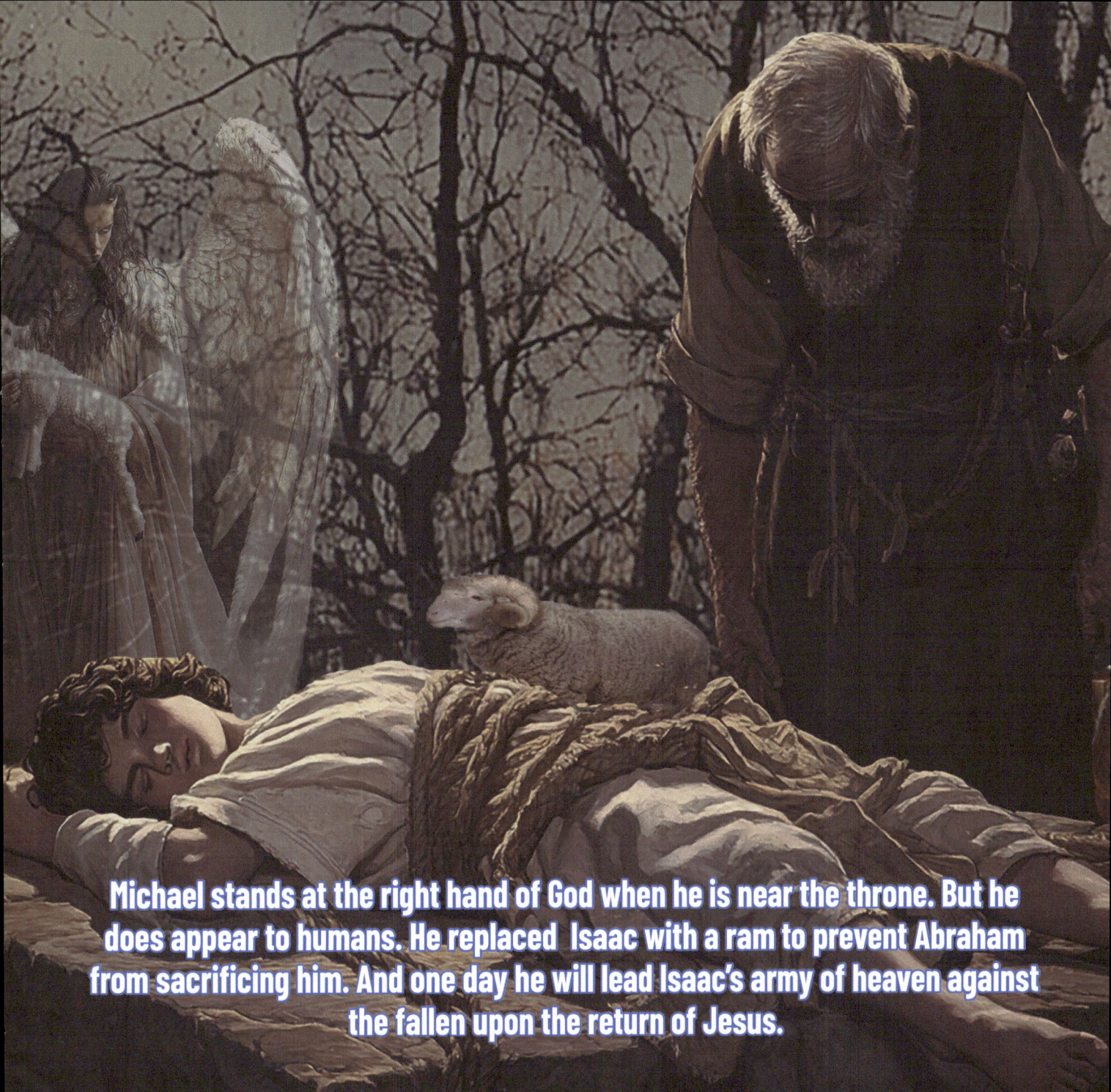

Michael stands at the right hand of God when he is near the throne. But he does appear to humans. He replaced Isaac with a ram to prevent Abraham from sacrificing him. And one day he will lead Isaac's army of heaven against the fallen upon the return of Jesus.

Raguel

As the archangel of justice, fairness & harmony, he maintains balance in the world. His name means Shepherd of God. He will deliver God's retribution upon those who have not followed God's laws as mentioned in the book of Revelation.

Raguel, principality archangel of the red horse and fiery sword, is said to be the second angel mentioned in the book of Revelation. When he blows his trumpet, a fiery mountain will strike the sea, killing a third of all life in and on the waters.

Raziel or Gallitsur is called the Keeper of Secrets, Mysteries and Revelations. He is said to provide the ability to clearly understand the lessons of the "Torah's Divine Wisdom."

Raziel is said to be one the three Archangels that visited Abraham. He is also said to be the angel who guided Adam and Eve after they were driven from the garden and helped them grow closer to God once again, and stories say he loved humans more than any other angel.

He is also known as the Angel of Magic. The Kabbalah credits him with taking God's divine secrets and writing them into a book of celestial and earthly knowledge. The book was given to Adam but stolen. Years later, Enoch found it and gave the book to Raphael who passed it on to Noah, and later to King Soloman.

As a high level seraphin Sandalphon is a member of the angelic armies that archangel Michael leads to fight Satan's armies.

Uriel

Also called Auriel and Oriel, he is the fourth Archangel and considered the angel of Wisdom and knowledge. His name means "God is my flame." Uriel is credited with spreading the light of truth to those who seek solutions and information.

Records name Uriel as the angel who guards the Tree of Wisdom after Adam and Eve were driven from Eden. During the first passover, Uriel is reported to be the angel that checked for blood on the door-frames and is also the angel that appeared to Noah and warned of the upcoming flood. Some say he will hold the key to the fiery pit in the end of times.

Zadkiel is said to comfort the sick and dying who have sinned and urges them to make things right between them and God before its too late. As the guardian of those who sleep in death he also encourages us to clear our soul and forgive those who have wronged us.

Zadkiel has been credited with visiting Abrahan before he moved to sacrifice Isaac. He is also thought to be the angel of the Lord in Genesis 22. Either way everyone agrees that he often prompts men to give their time and money to charitable acts.

Samyaza, Azazel, Azza & Uzza

Don't make the mistake of thinking the fallen are all ugly misshapen demons, as they were all angels that were cast out of heaven with Lucifer for sinning against God. Many of the most wicked are extremely attractive, and use deception to achieve their goals.

Satan

Lucifer Morningstar or the great deceiver, was once known as the greatest of God's creations. He fell victim to his own ego & pride and was expelled from Heaven for sin against God. He seduces humans into sin or falsehood with the other fallen angels aka demons.

SALVATION PRAYER

God, I know I sinned against you. Forgive me for the wrong that I have done. I believe that Jesus Christ died on the cross for me. That He rose from the grave so that after three days. I can have His long-lasting life. Come into my heart to be my Lord and Savior. I choose to turn away from my sins and I choose to follow you. Lead me to walk with you. Keep me safe and teach me your ways. Stop every bad thing in my life that has an open door to hurt me. Close those doors. Holy Spirit fill me now in Jesus' name. Amen.

BAPTISM IN THE HOLY SPIRIT

Jesus, you are the one that fills me with Your Spirit. Come Holy Spirit and come into my life and fill me to overflow with Your presence. Come with your fire too. Thank you for the gift of tongues in Jesus' name. Amen.

Open your mouth and let the words come out that God gives you. It will be words that you don't know what they mean. You can ask God what it means. You need to let Him talk through you every day to grow this gift.

He will bring you closer to God and you will know Jesus more. You will have power from God to do great things and know things.

PRAYER

Thank you, Father, for sending your angels to help me. Thank you for the different angels in this book. Teach me how to command them using your. words. I pray for my angels to always protect me and to guide me on the right path. Teach me how to follow you every day. Teach me how to fight the enemy with your words. Help me see my angels and to work with them in Jesus' name. Amen.

Message from the Author

Thank you for reading this book. I hope you can leave a good review to encourage me to write more books to teach children and adults. We can get to know our angels, we remember that they serve God first. Then the animals serve us. We are not to worship them, but to obey God's message and to command them to do God's work. Angels follow us wherever we go. They have to go with us. They are not everywhere all the time, like God, Jesus, and the Holy Spirit. The Lord has given us angels to watch over us all the time. Angels can bring us to heaven and hell to show us what God wants us to see and know. There are angels will visit us and they will tell us what we need to do and we need to listen and do what they tell us.

OTHER PRODUCTS

- Knowing God
- How to Hear God's Voice
- New Life in Jesus
- Loving Israel
- God's Gifts/Spiritual Talents
- Meeting God
- Word Power
- Fruit of the Spirit
- The Tabernacle
- Bride for Jesus
- A Life of Prayer
- Live Free
- Who am I in Jesus
- Walk in Love
- God's Favor
- Man of God
- Woman of God
- How to Use Money
- God's Wisdom
- Fasting
- See Jerusalem and Bethany
- First Fruit Offering
- Feast of Trumpets
- Day of Atonement
- Feast of Tabernacles
- Counting the Omer
- Festival of Lights
- Glory, Presence, and Holy Spirit
- Live in God's Presence
- Pentecost
- See Galilee, Nazareth, and Tiberias
- Hear God Speak
- Knowing Jesus
- Knowing Holy Spirit
- A Healthy Life and Healthy Life Work Book
- Smokey the Cat
- Passover Unleavened Bread
- Resurrection Life
- The Blessing
- Revival
- Chelsea Learns Hebrew
- Thanksgiving
- Give Thanks
- Jesus Birth
- Loving Jesus: Bride and Groom
- Proverbs 31 Woman

OTHER PRODUCTS

ABC of People in the Bible
Colours in the Bible
Breakthroughs
Open Doors
The Seven Spirits of God
Numbers in the Bible
Aglee the Eagle
An Eagle's Life
ABC's of Faith

Devotionals
31 Day Devotional

Inspirational/Other
Chelsea's Psalms and Poems
Your Daily Meal: Chelsea's Photo Album

Puzzle Books
Biblical Puzzle Book Vol 1-5
Bible Puzzles for Young Children Book 1-3
Biblical Puzzle for Children Books 1-5

Teaching Series
How to Hear God's Voice Teaching Guide & Audio Book
Relationship with God, Jesus, Holy Spirit Guide
Knowing God, Jesus, Holy Spirit Guide & Audio Book
Flowing in the Prophetic

Teaching (Non-Sale on my website)
Purim
Passover
Resurrection

BOOK REVIEWS

More books on Amazon, Kobo, and Barnes and Noble, Smashwords, and IngramSpark.
https://chelseak532002550.wordpress.com/

More books on Amazon, Kobo, and Barnes and Noble, Smashwords, and IngramSpark.
https://www.amazon.com/author/chelseakong

Please leave a review and share with friends to help the author continue to write more books to reach more readers. Thank you so much for your support.

Review!

COACHING PRODUCTS

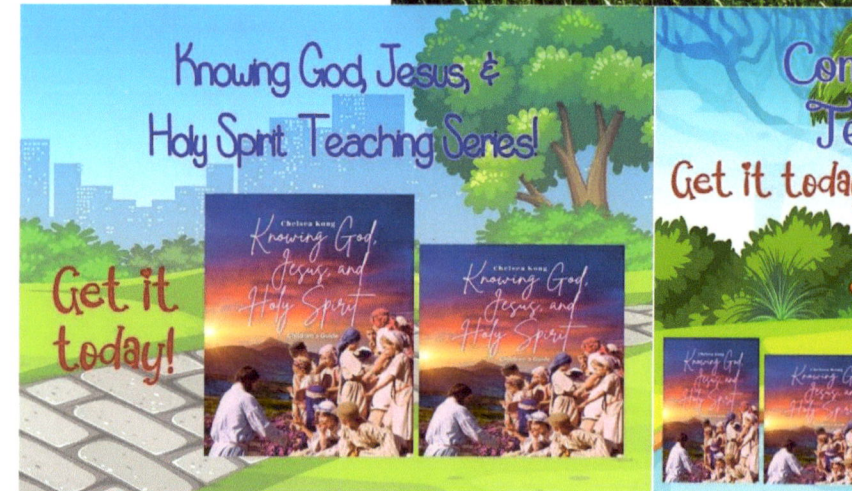
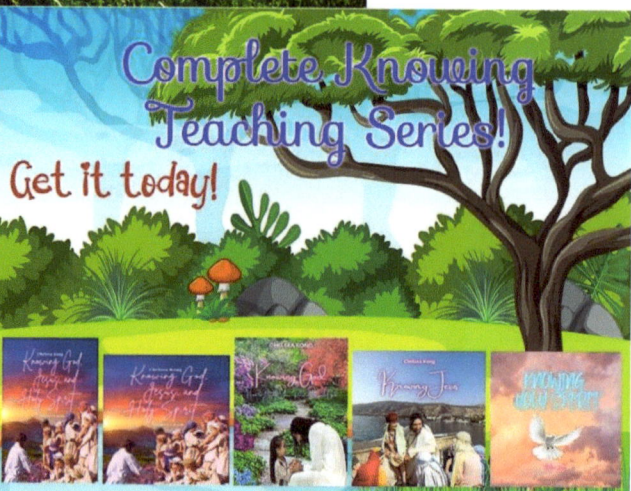

Great books for children. You can get the books individually through Amazon and Barnes and Noble.
https://chelseak532002550.wordpress.com/

COACHING PRODUCTS

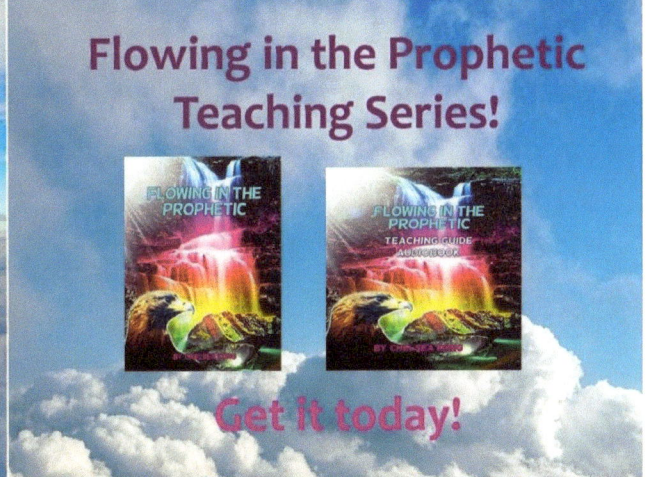

Great books for adults.
You can get the books individually through Amazon.
https://chelseak532002550.wordpress.com/

More books coming!

About
CHELSEA KONG

She is a writer, creative arts and digital media artist, skilled administration and payroll professional, and podcaster. Chelsea also served in a variety of roles, from audiovisual, photography, to assisting on the worship team, and ministry team. She also has a passion for families being united.

Chelsea has been a guest on Unity Live Radio, The Lady Tracey Show, and How to Live for Christ and is highly recommended by a Proud Christian blog. She is also a guest blogger. A few of her books have been featured in YourAuthorHub, etc. She graduated from Hotel and Restaurant Management, Digital Media Arts, Office Administration, Payroll Professional, and experience working with children. Chelsea lives in Toronto, Canada. She mainly writes children's books, stories, bridal writing, poems, lyrics for songs, words of encouragement, blessings, prayers, and jokes. The author of How to Hear the Voice of God, the Bridal Collection, Knowing God, etc. She also has her own Bible Puzzle books and other inspired products. Her podcast channel is called Chelsea K on Anchor, Spotify, and iTunes.

Please check my website to find out more:
https://chelseak532002550.wordpress.com/

www.ingramcontent.com/pod-product-compliance
Lightning Source LLC
Chambersburg PA
CBHW042054050526
44107CB00110B/1150